Meaningful Mathematics
Level 1:

Activity-based Learning Book for Children Ages 4, 5 and 6 Years Old

Name: _______________________________

Class : _______________________________

Age : _______________________________

Little Ones Meaningful Mathematics Level 1:
Activity-based Learning Book for Children Ages 4, 5 and 6 Years Old

Advisor
Dr. Mohd Fauzi Shaffie
DBA (MMU), MBA (UiTM), BSc(H) Physics (Cardiff University, U.K.)

Writer
Wan Roslina Wan Yusoff
MA in Human Developmental Psychology (UKM)
BSc(H) Physics (Cardiff University, U.K.)

Creative Director
Abdullah Munzir Mohd Fauzi

Co-Editor
Rosmaizura Muhamad

Graphics
Lee Ee Bing
Mohd Norfahmy Mohd Ismail

Original Concept For Illustrations
Abdussalaam Syaahid Mohd Fauzi

Design & Layout
MZR Global Sdn Bhd

Publisher
Little Ones International Sdn Bhd
No. 5A, 1st Floor, Jalan Kristal K7/K, Seksyen 7,
40000 Shah Alam, Selangor, Malaysia.

www.littleones.my

ISBN 978-967-14052-5-3

First Edition 2017

Contents

Little Ones™ Meaningful Mathematics

Level 1, 2 and 3 of the Little Ones Meaningful Mathematics books are based on the 6 themes found in both the Little Ones™ English and Little Ones™ Adventurous Science. The themes are:

1. At Home
2. The Toys
3. In the Garden
4. In a Shop
5. At the Play School
6. At School

With more vocabulary introduced and systematic step-by-step procedures in hands-on experiments, children as young as 3 years old are taught to observe and record their observations in the Little Ones™ Meaningful Mathematics modules.

Special instructional and explanation words are repeated to enchance the understanding and usage of Mathematical Language.

Workshops

Special workshops for the Little Ones™ Meaningful Mathematics are held regulary to help teachers and parents acquire the skills of teaching Mathematics to the preschool children.

At the end of the workshops, participants will:

1. Understand the psychological factor of children developing cognitively.
2. Know the vocabulary words to be taught for each topic.
3. Learn the mathematical concepts and the methods to teach them.
4. Acquire the skills to handle the children in carrying out explorations.
5. Learn the instructions and explanations to be given to the children.
6. Get suggestions and guidance in planning the lesson plans.

Teachers and parents who have gone through the workshop find the Little Ones™ Meaningful Mathematics modules helpful in building up good Mathematical skills among the preschool children.

LOE: 5 Ex-Learning Approach

Let the children:

Little Ones Eduworld Meaningful Mathematics Level 1:
Activity-based Learning Book for Children Ages 4, 5 and 6 Years Old
Little Ones Eduworld

CONCEPT: GROUPING

1. Myself

Date: _________

Objective:

To know and count parts of the body which are groups of I.

Method:

Teacher shows and says parts of the body which are I. Colour the numbers I below.
Sing the song "Head, shoulders, knees and toes".

Say: I have ____

I head

I face

I nose

I mouth

Mouth	Nose	Head

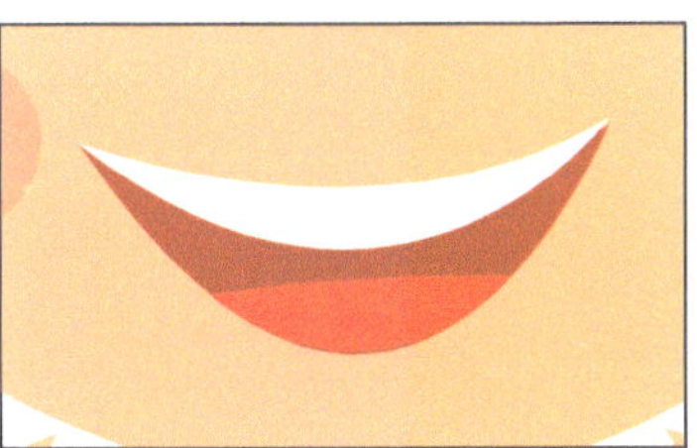 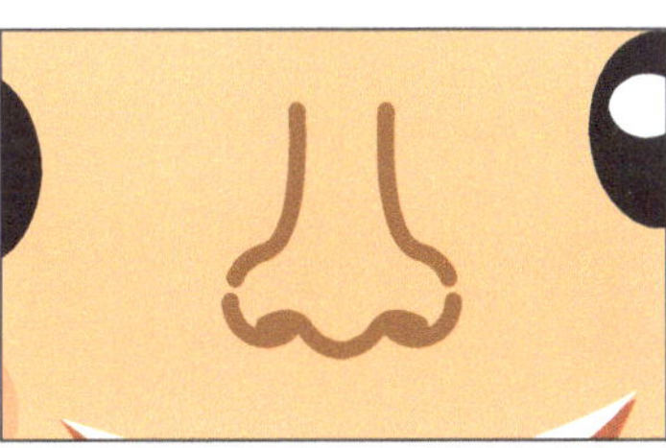 

2. Myself

Date: _______________

Objective:
To know and count parts of the body which are groups of 2.

Method:
Teacher shows and says parts of the body which are 2. Colour the numbers 2 below.

Say: I have ____

2 eyes

2 ears

2 hands

2 legs

2 feet

Eyes

Legs

Hands

Little Ones Eduworld Meaningful Mathematics Level 1:
Activity-based Learning Book for Children Ages 4, 5 and 6 Years Old

Little Ones Eduworld

3. Myself

Date: _________

Paste a picture of myself (One)(Choose from the sticker page).

Picture of myself.

Myself and my friend

Paste a picture of myself and my friend (Two) (Choose from the sticker page).

Picture of myself and friend.

4. Parts of the body

Date: _______________

Match the numbers to the quantities.

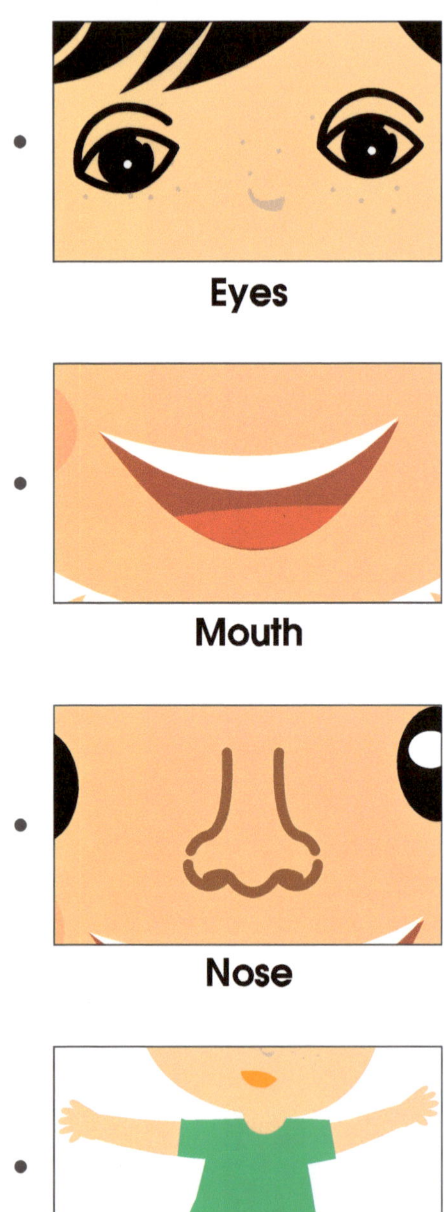

Little Ones Eduworld Meaningful Mathematics Level 1: *Activity-based Learning Book for Children Ages 4, 5 and 6 Years Old* Little Ones Eduworld

5. Things in the kitchen   Date: __________

Objective:
To introduce the names of the things in the kitchen and pairing them with
(i) the things of the same shapes (ii) the same things.

Method:
Teacher shows things as in the pictures below.
1. Pair the same shapes of the plates.
2. Pair the same things in the kitchen
3. Pairing same shapes and sizes.

1. Pairing same shapes and sizes

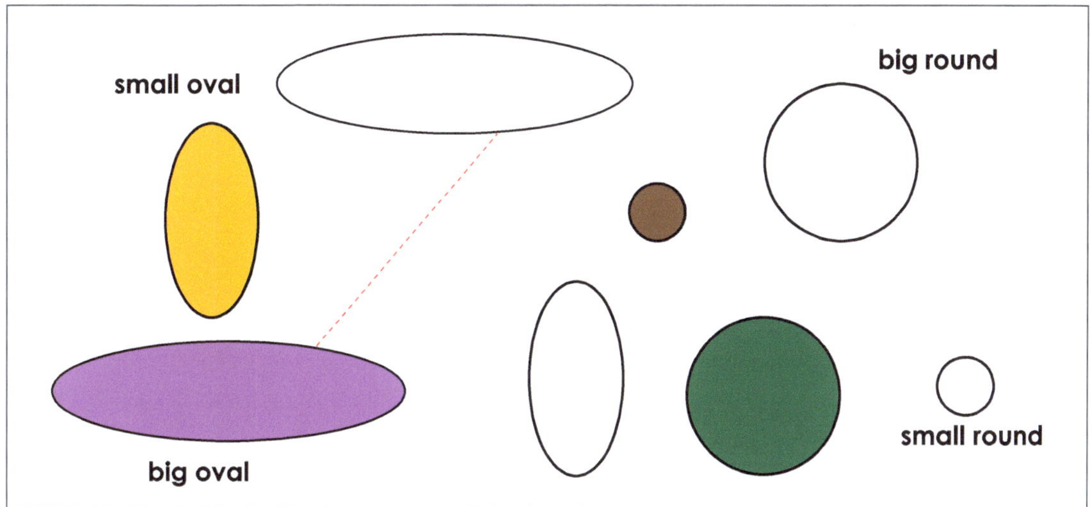

2. Pairing same things.

6. Round & oval plates

Date: _____________

Paste the sticker of one big round plate.

| big round plate

Paste the stickers of two small oval plates.

2 small oval plates

7. Round & oval plates

Date: _________

Paste the stickers below.

round	round
☐ small round plate	☐ big round plate
oval	**oval**
☐ small oval plate	☐ big oval plate

small   big

8. Same things in the kitchen.

Date: ___________

Paste the stickers below.

same

| knife | knife |

same

2 forks 2 forks

CONCEPT: GROUPING

9. Cloth Pegs

Date: _____________

Objective:
To group items according to the colours.

Method:
1. Teacher prepares cloth pegs with different colours for children to group them.
2. Place 20 cloth pegs in a container. (5 pieces for each colour)
3. Prepare different containers for different colours, paste coloured papers on the containers.
4. Let each child take 1 peg and put it inside the container with the same colours.
5. Say "1 group of red pegs ...."

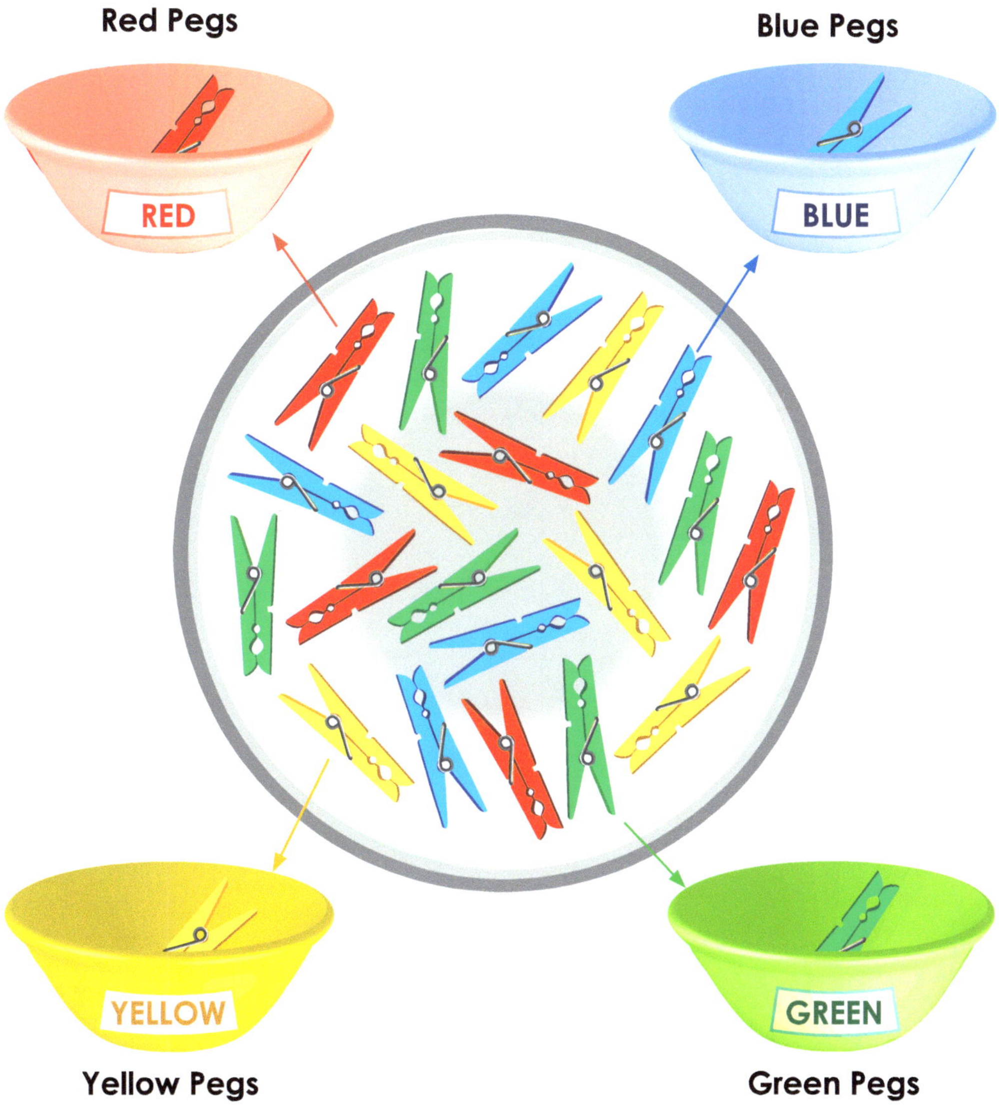

Red Pegs

Blue Pegs

Yellow Pegs

Green Pegs

10. Group of coloured pegs

Date: __________

Paste the stickers of the pegs according to the colours.

2 Red pegs	2 Blue pegs
2 Green pegs	2 Yellow pegs

11. Balls

Date: _________

Objective:
To count until 3 objects.

Method:
Teacher shows the objects and the number card ⬚3⬚ . Then, count the pictures and trace the numbers.

(3) Footballs

(3) Balls

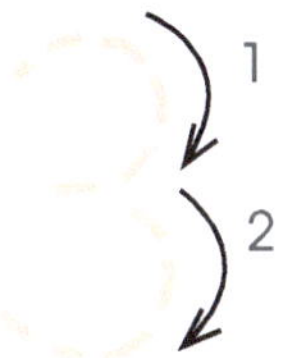

(3) Tennis balls

(3) Ping pong balls

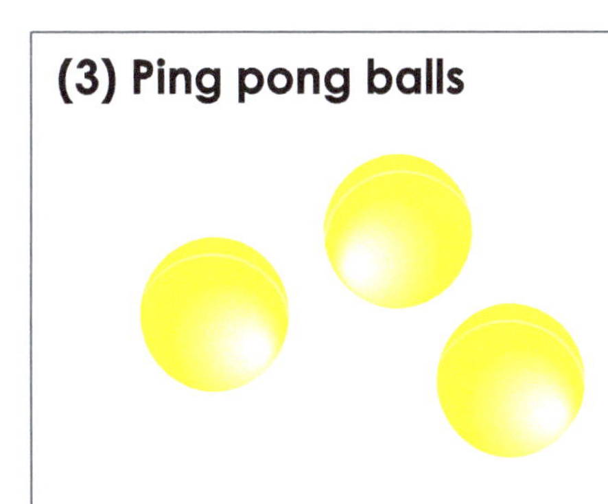

12. The toy vehicles

Date: ___________

Objective:
To name some of the toy vehicles, and to count and match symbols with quantities until three.

Method:
Teacher shows the different toy vehicles available. Use number cards 1, 2 and 3. Count, trace, and then colour the numbers and the pictures.

Which **toy vehicle** do you like?

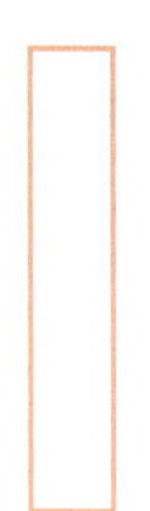

13. The Toy vehicles

Date: _______________

Paste the toy vehicle stickers according to the numbers.

<table>
<tr><td>

1 truck

</td><td>

2 cars

</td></tr>
<tr><td colspan="2">

3 boats

</td></tr>
</table>

14. The soft toys

Date: ___________

Objectice:
To name some of the soft toys available and to count and match symbols with quantities of four.

Method:
Teacher shows the soft toys. Count and match number cards to the quantities. Count, trace, and then colour the pictures.

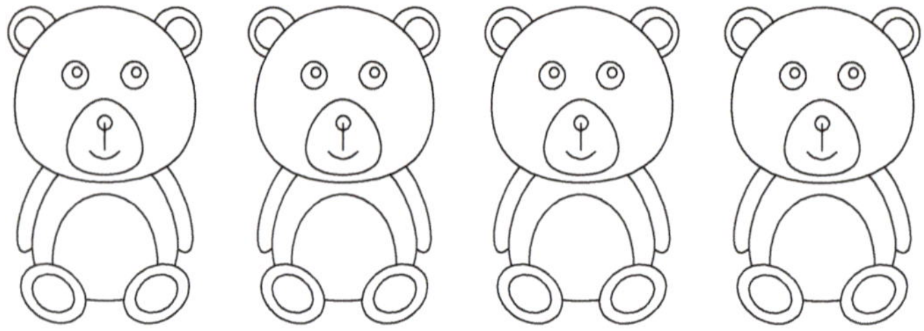

Teddy bears

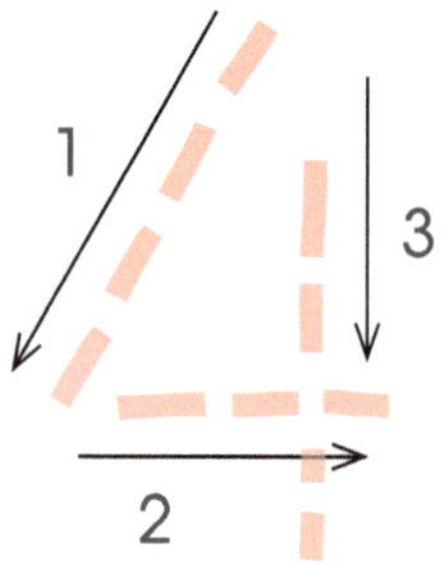

Ducks

Kittens

15. The soft toys

Date: _________

Paste the stickers of the soft toys.

1 Crocodile

2 Hens

3 Ducks

4 Teddy bears

MATCHING QUANTITIES - SYMBOLS

16. Toys

Date: __________

Match the quantities to the numbers.

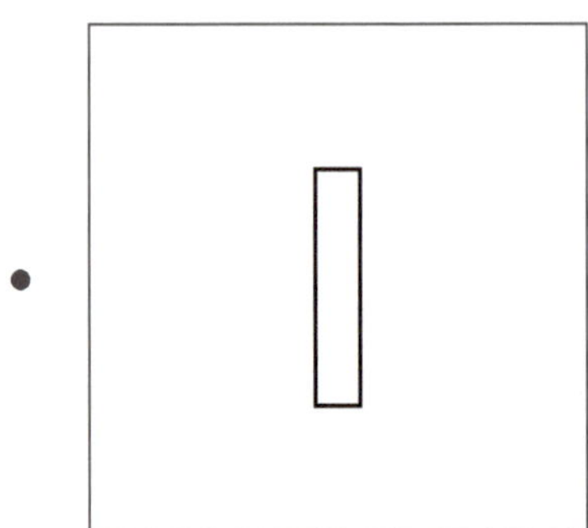

Little Ones Eduworld Meaningful Mathematics Level 1:
Activity-based Learning Book for Children Ages 4, 5 and 6 Years Old

17. Numbers

Date: _________

Write numbers 1 until 4

1

2

3

4

18. Toys

Date: __________

Match the numbers to quantities.

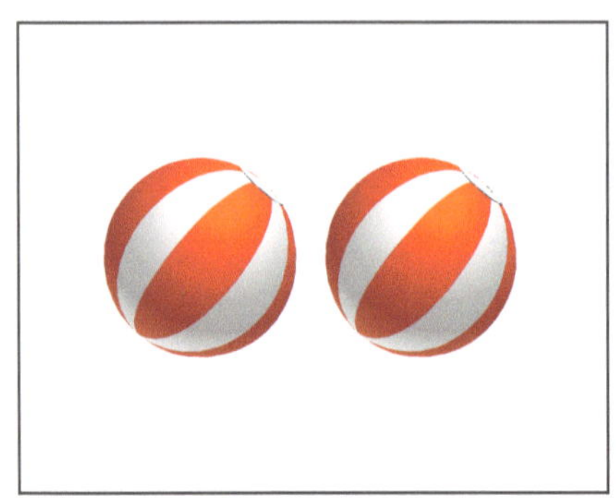

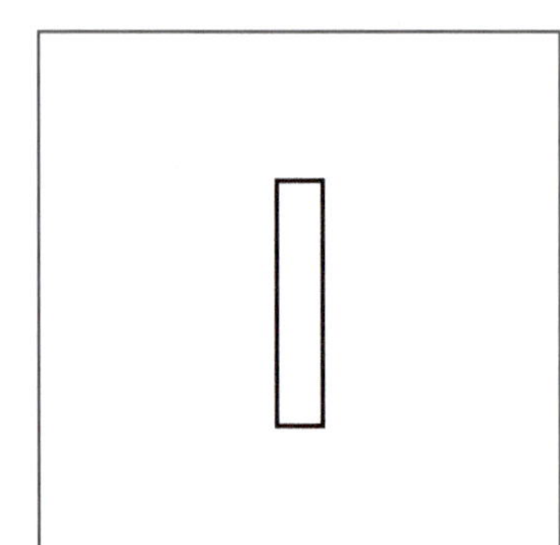

19. Trees

Date: _____________

Objective:

To introduce the words short and tall trees.

Method:

Teacher brings the children out and shows the short and tall trees. Count the pictures. Trace the numbers.

Short trees

Tall trees

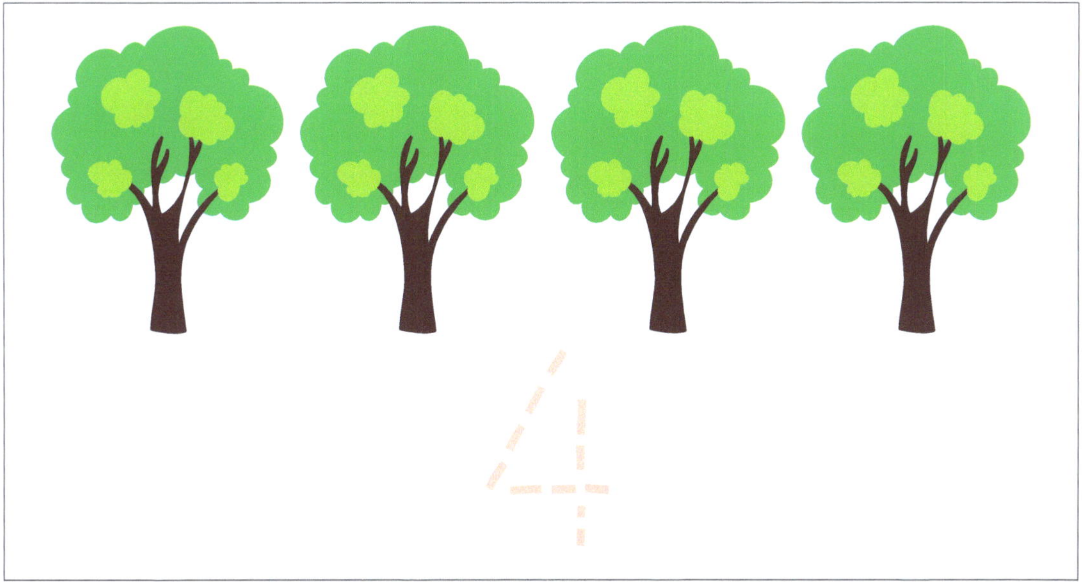

20. Plants

Date: _____________

Paste the stickers accordingly.

Short Plant	Tall Tree
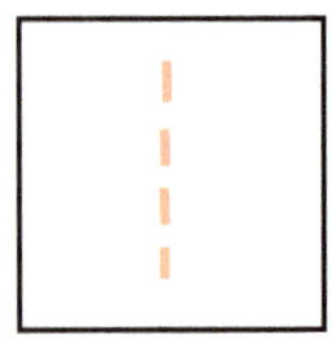	
Short Plants	Tall Trees

Little Ones Eduworld Meaningful Mathematics Level 1:
Activity-based Learning Book for Children Ages 4, 5 and 6 Years Old

Little Ones Eduworld

CONCEPT: MEASUREMENT

21. Leaves

Date: ___________

Objective:
To introduce the words big and small and to count until five.

Method:
Teacher brings the children out to collect different shapes of leaves. Group them into small and big leaves. Count the leaves in groups of five.

Are the leaves small? How many are there? Colour the leaves.

Are the leaves big? How many are there? Colour the leaves.

22. Leaves

Date: _________

Paste 5 small leaves and 5 big leaves from the stickers on sticker page.

Small leaves

____

Big leaves

WRITING

23. Numbers Four & Five   Date: __________

Write the numbers 4 and 5.

4			
4			
4			
5			
5			
5			

24. Stones (1 until 5)   Date: _______

Objective:
To reinforce the matching of number symbols and their quantities.

Method:
Teacher uses number cards and stones for matching. Children paste the number stickers according to the quantities.

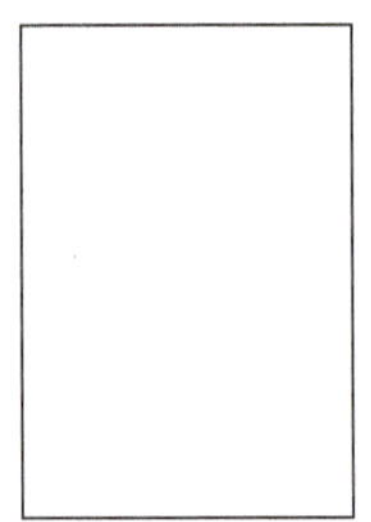

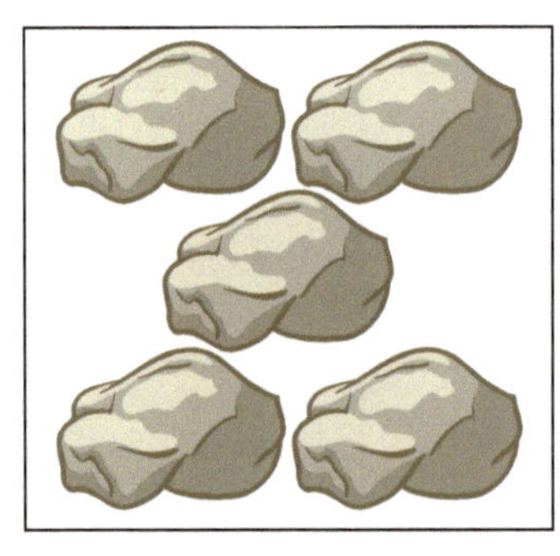

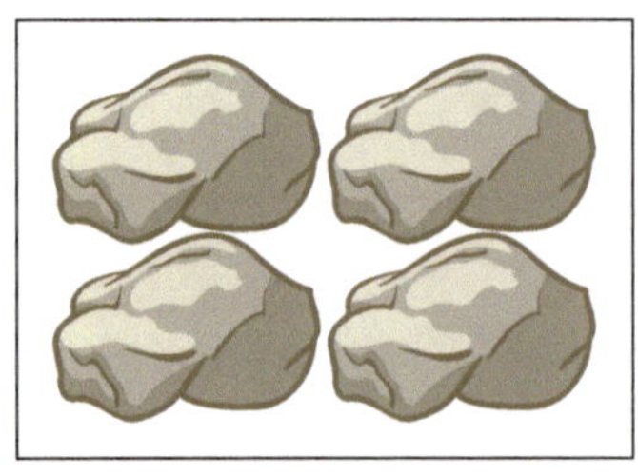

Little Ones Eduworld Meaningful Mathematics Level 1:
Activity-based Learning Book for Children Ages 4, 5 and 6 Years Old

25. Stones

Date: _________

Paste the stickers of stones according to the number symbols.

1

2

3

4

26. Marbles

Date: _______

Objective:

Teacher checks each child for matching number symbols to the correct quantities.

Method:

Using 5 marbles and number cards 1 until 5 , circle the correct number of marbles.
Asks each child to match quantities to number symbols.

1	4	3	2	1	3

5	1	3	2	5	4

Little Ones Eduworld Meaningful Mathematics Level 1:
Activity-based Learning Book for Children Ages 4, 5 and 6 Years Old
Little Ones Eduworld

Revision

Date: _______________

Match the quantities to the numbers. Colour the numbers.

 •   • 

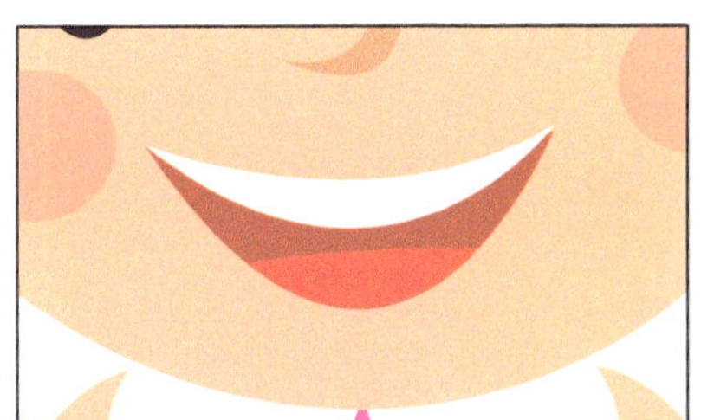 •   • 

 •   • 

 •   • 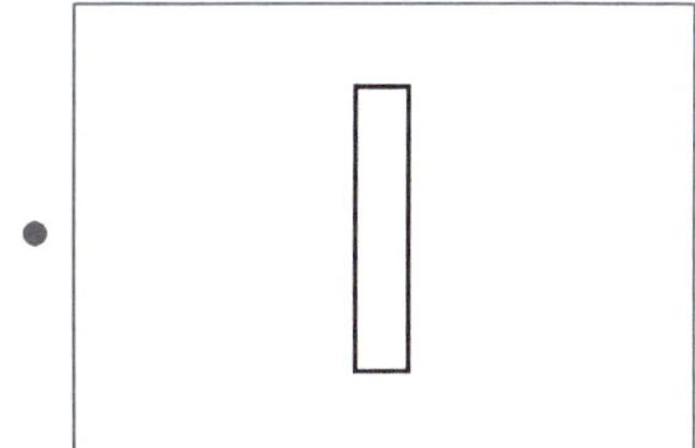

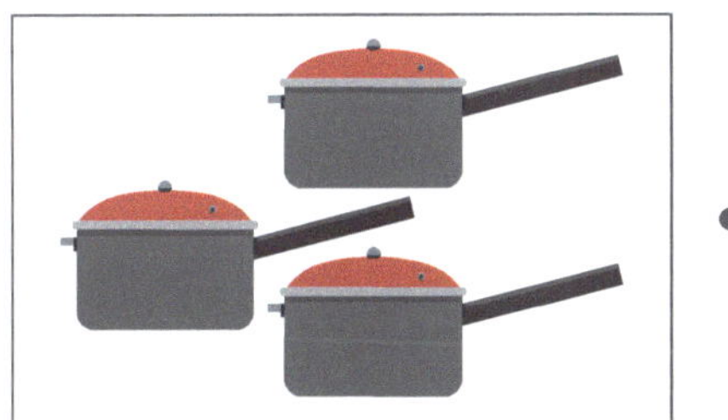 •   • 5

27. Home animals

Date: ___________

Objective:
To name some of the animals found in our homes.
To teach 'more than' concept using matching 'one-to-one' method.

Method:
Teacher uses models of the animals.
Example: Number 1 cat is for number 1 dog. (Join the dotted line).
Number 2 cat has NO dog. Why? Because 2 cats are ⟩ **More than** ⟩ 1 dog.

Cats

Dog

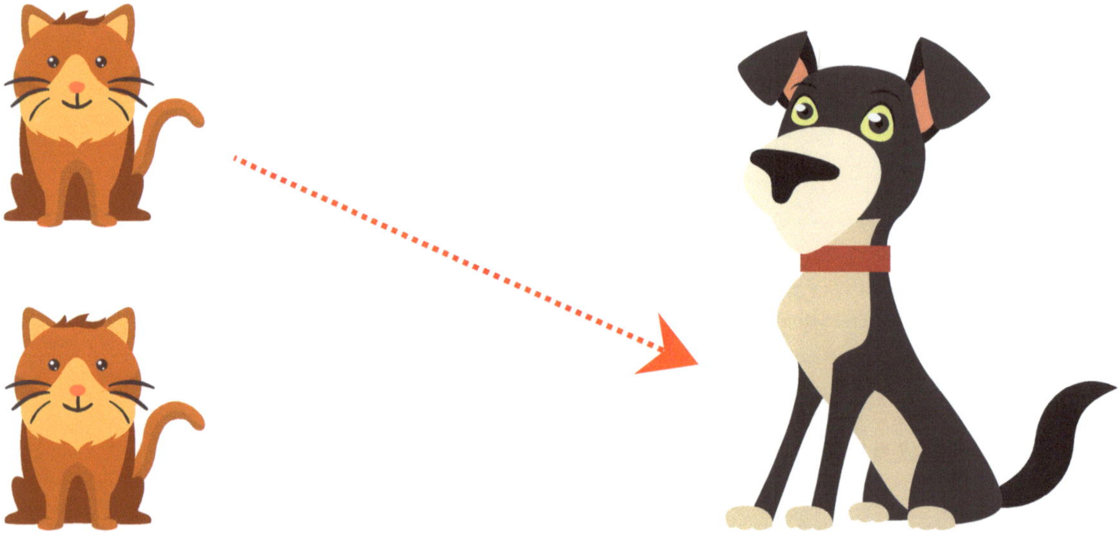

More than

CONCEPT: 'MORE THAN'

28. Pets

Date: _____________

Objective:
To name the pets at home.
To teach 'more than' concept using matching 'one-to-one' method.

Method:
Teacher uses models of fishes and tortoises.
Example: Number 1 fish is for number 1 tortoise.
Number 2 fish is for number 2 tortoise.
Number 3 fish has NO tortoise. Why? Because 3 fishes are **More than** 2 tortoises.

Fish   Tortoises

CONCEPT: 'MORE THAN'

29. Farm animals

Date: _______________

Method:
Count and match the animals to show 'more than' concept.

Ducklings

Duck

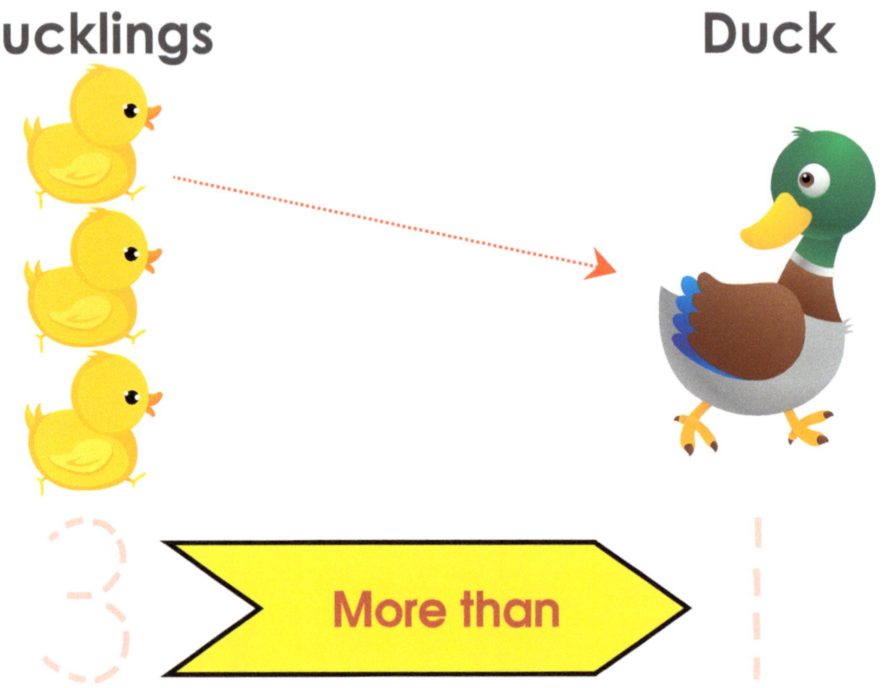

Kids

Goats

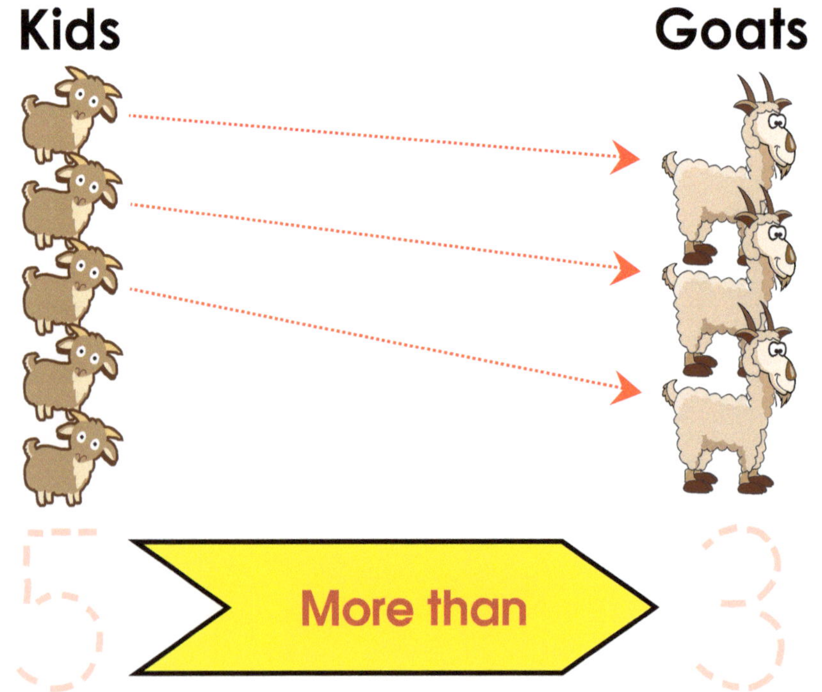

Little Ones Eduworld Meaningful Mathematics Level 1:
Activity-based Learning Book for Children Ages 4, 5 and 6 Years Old

Little Ones Eduworld

CONCEPT: 'MORE THAN'

30. Vegetables

Date: _______________

Method:
Teacher uses the vegetables (models or real) to match for > **More than** > concept using 'one-to-one' matching method. Join the dotted lines below.

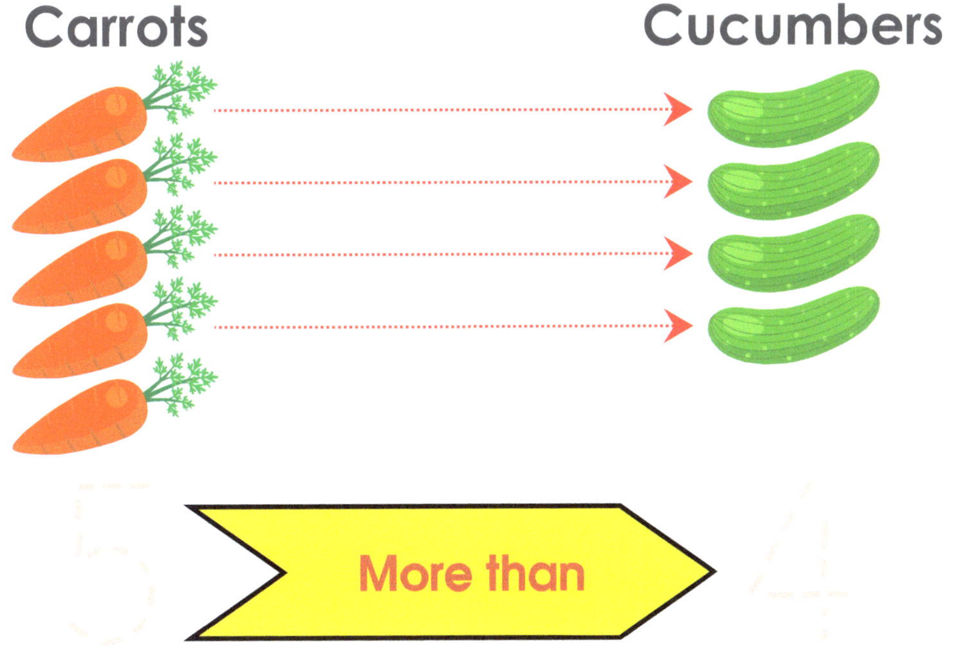

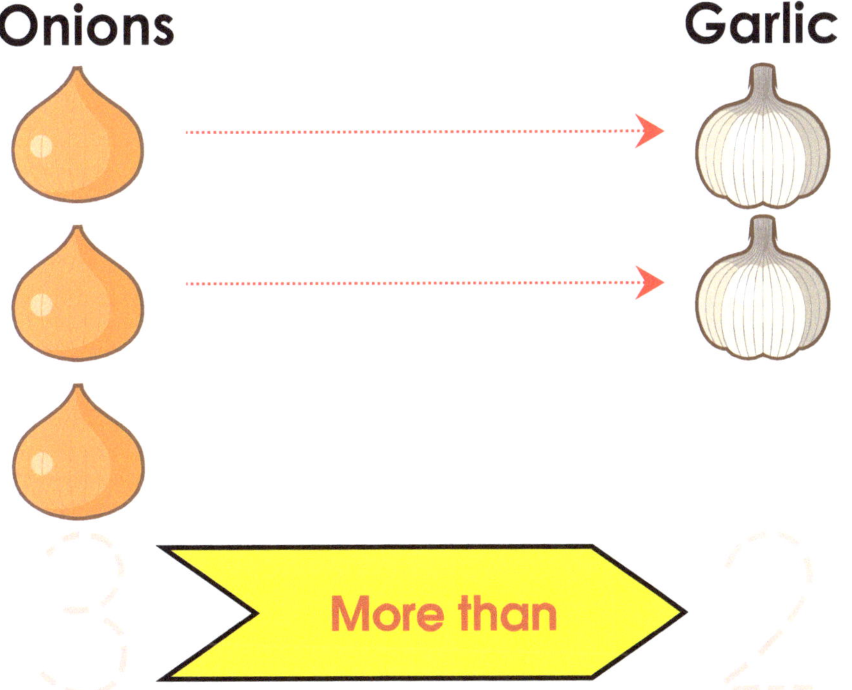

CONCEPT: 'MORE THAN'

31. Fruits

Date: ___________

Method:
Teacher prepares apples, oranges and bananas (real or models). Number cards 1 until 5. Let children match using 'one-to-one' method for the 'more than' concept.

Exercise:
Count the fruits and colour the correct numbers for the 'more than' concept.

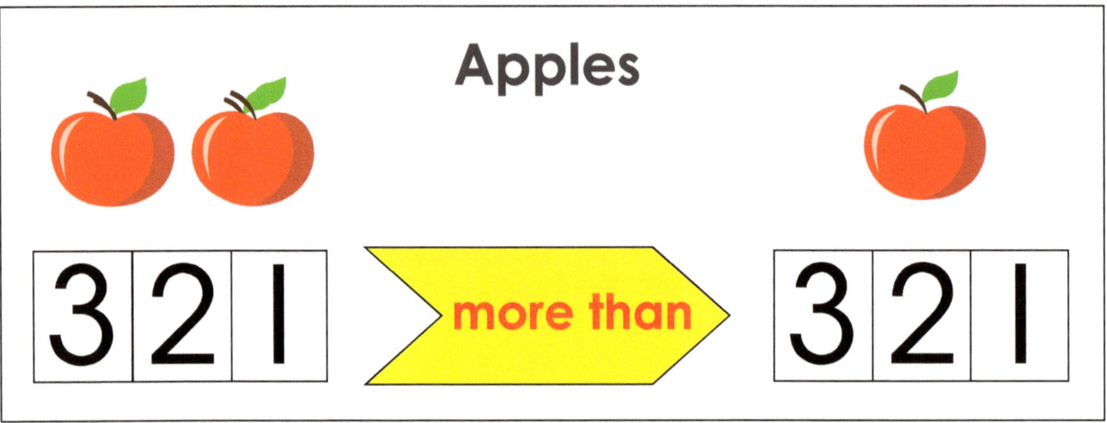

Little Ones Eduworld Meaningful Mathematics Level 1:
Activity-based Learning Book for Children Ages 4, 5 and 6 Years Old
Little Ones Eduworld

In The Garden

CONCEPT: LIGHT & HEAVY

32. Sand

Date: ___________

Objective:
To introduce concepts of light, heavy and more than. Experience weighing things. Heavy objects needle moves **More than** light objects.

Method:
Teacher prepares 5 packets of sand of equal weights (about 20 grams each). Show to the children then compare the weights using 2 weighing machines (show the needle readings)

Heavy   **Light**

2 **More than** **1**

bottles   bottle

Heavy   **Light**

3 **More than** **2**

bottles   bottles

33. Sand

Date: _______________

Paste pictures of bottles of sand on the appropriate weighing machines. Colour the numbers 1 & 2 and the 'more than' symbol.

34. Shaping the Numbers   Date: _______

Objective:

To feel the shapes and directions of forming numbers.

Method:

Teacher asks children to put glue inside the numbers. Then paste punched coloured papers following directions of the shapes of the numbers.

35. Number One until Five   Date: __________

Practise writing the numbers 1 until 5

1	1	1	1	1	1
2	2	2	2	2	2
3	3	3	3	3	3
4	4	4	4	4	4
5	5	5	5	5	5

CONCEPT: ADD ONE MORE

36. Magnetic Buttons   Date: __________

Objective:
To teach children the symbol `+` (add) by adding one more to the objects (within 1 to 5 objects).

Method:

Teacher arranges the number cards `1` until `5` on a magnetic whiteboard. Say out the number cards with the children.

Place one black button under the number `1` card. Teacher asks: "how many buttons?" Children answer: "one"

Show the `+` add card. Place a red button to the black button. Say "Add one more". Teacher asks: "how many buttons now?". Children count: "two".

Teacher asks: "is this number `2`?". Children say: "No". Teacher asks: "Where is number `2`?". Children say: "there, near `1`". Teacher says: "Let's move the two buttons to number `2` card".

Now repeat the steps `3` & `4` above until the total number of buttons are `5` and placed under the number `5` card.

Let each child do this "add one more" concept using the `+` card with teacher's guidance (experiential learning).

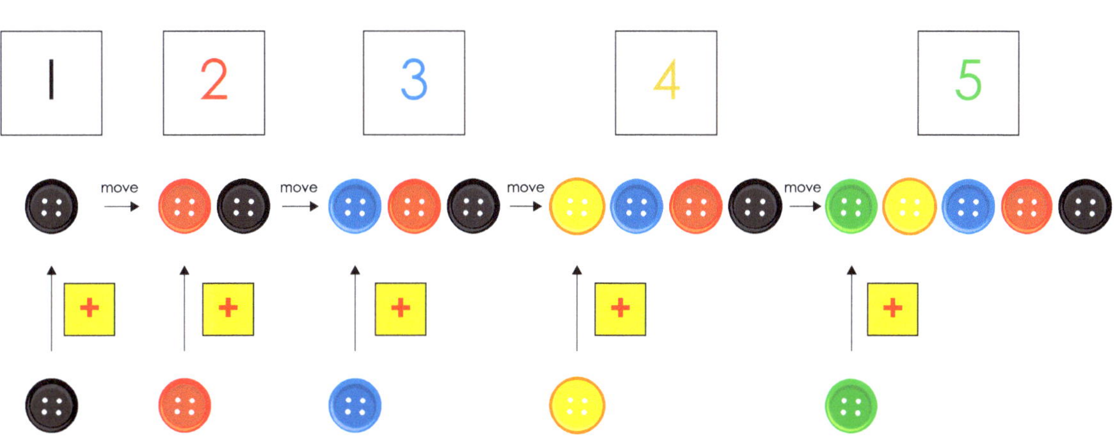

CONCEPT: ADD ONE MORE

37. Round stickers

Date: _____________

Method:
Paste round stickers on the round pictures. Trace the total numbers.

◯	✚	◯	=	2
1	add	1	equals	

◯◯	✚	◯	=	3
2	add	1	equals	

◯◯◯	✚	◯	=	4
3	add	1	equals	

◯◯◯◯	✚	◯	=	5
4	add	1	equals	

Little Ones Eduworld Meaningful Mathematics Level 1:
Activity-based Learning Book for Children Ages 4, 5 and 6 Years Old

CONCEPT: ADD ONE MORE

38. Plastic Flowers

Date: _________

Objective:

To introduce objects of 6 by adding one more.

Method:

Teacher shows the plastic stalks of flowers. Start counting from 1 flower until 5. Introduce 'add one more' to '5', now we have 6 flowers.

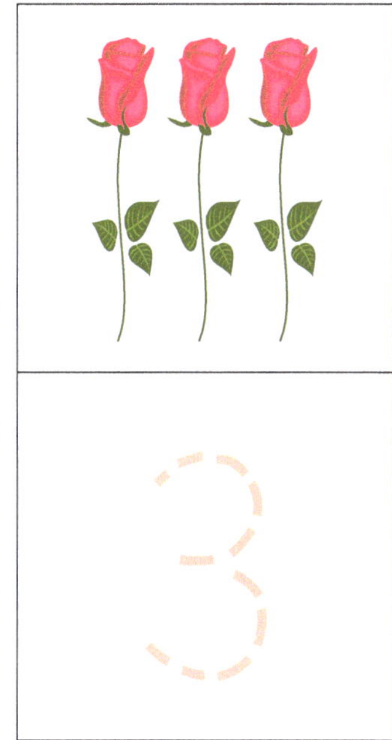

39. Flowers

Date: _________

Objective:
Add one more to make 6 flowers.

Method:
Paste the pictures stickers of the flowers according to the numbers.

1	2	3
4	5	6

CONCEPT: GROUPS OF 6

40. Basket

Date: _____________

Objective:

To show groups of 6 for different objects found in a flower shop.

Method:

Teacher displays different baskets, plastic leaves, vases in groups of 6. Ask the children to count and match with the number card 6. Trace the numbers.

41. Stationery

Date: _______________

Objective:
To introduce number 7 using the concept of "add one more".

Method:
Teacher groups the stationery into groups of 6. Show the number card 6. Then using the add ⊞ card, put one more object to the group 6. Say "6 add one more equals 7".

Do the same step for the other objects.

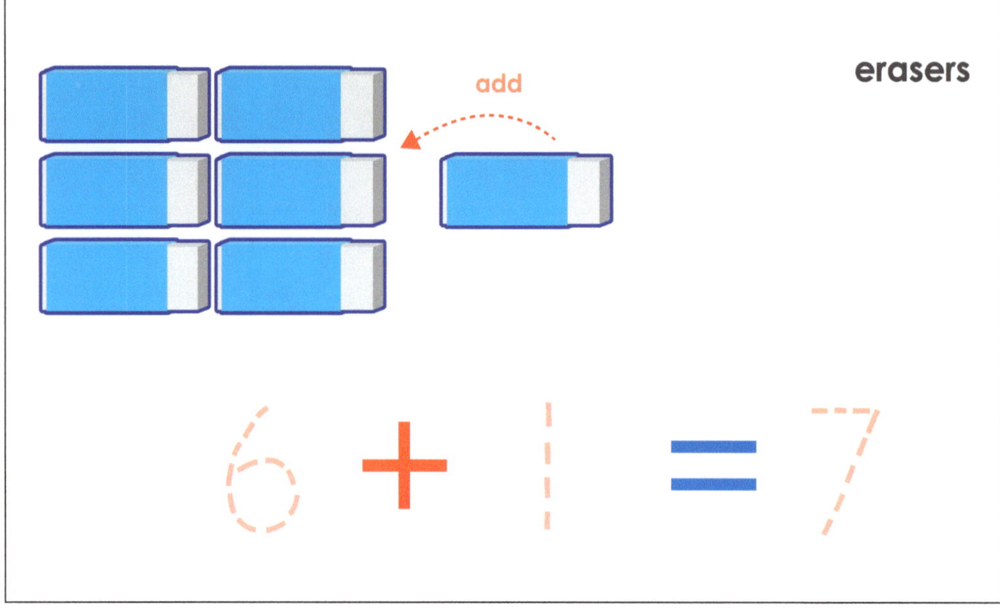

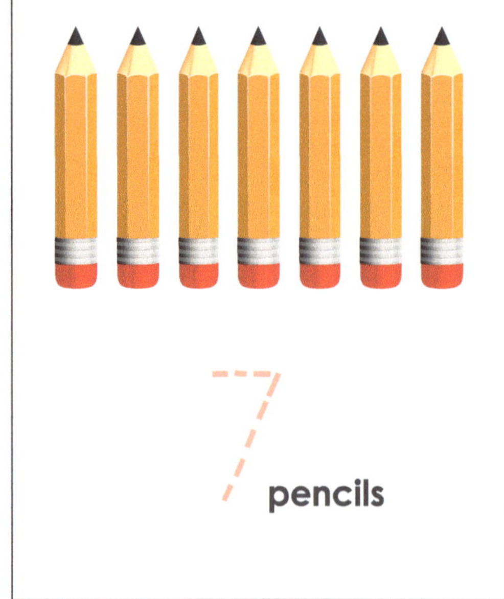

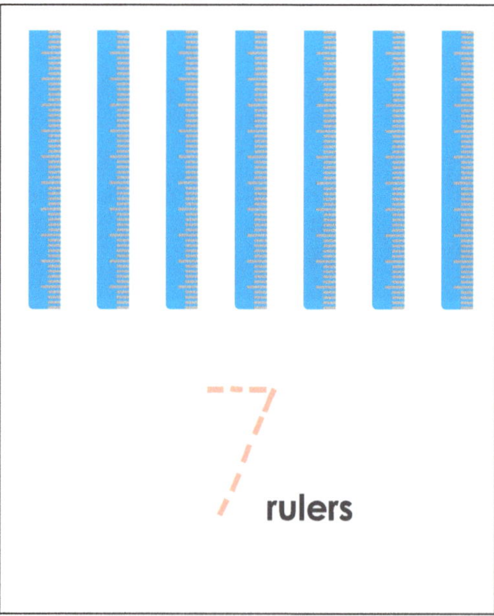

42. Stationery

Date: ________

Paste the stickers of the erasers as shown in the boxes.

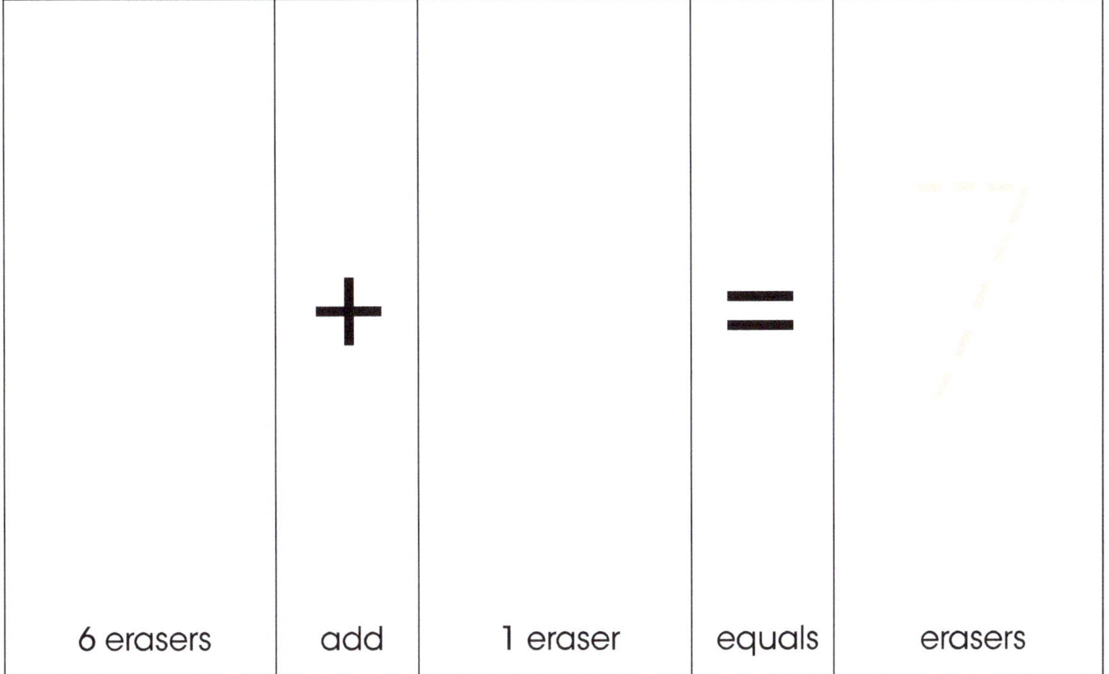

Write the number 7.

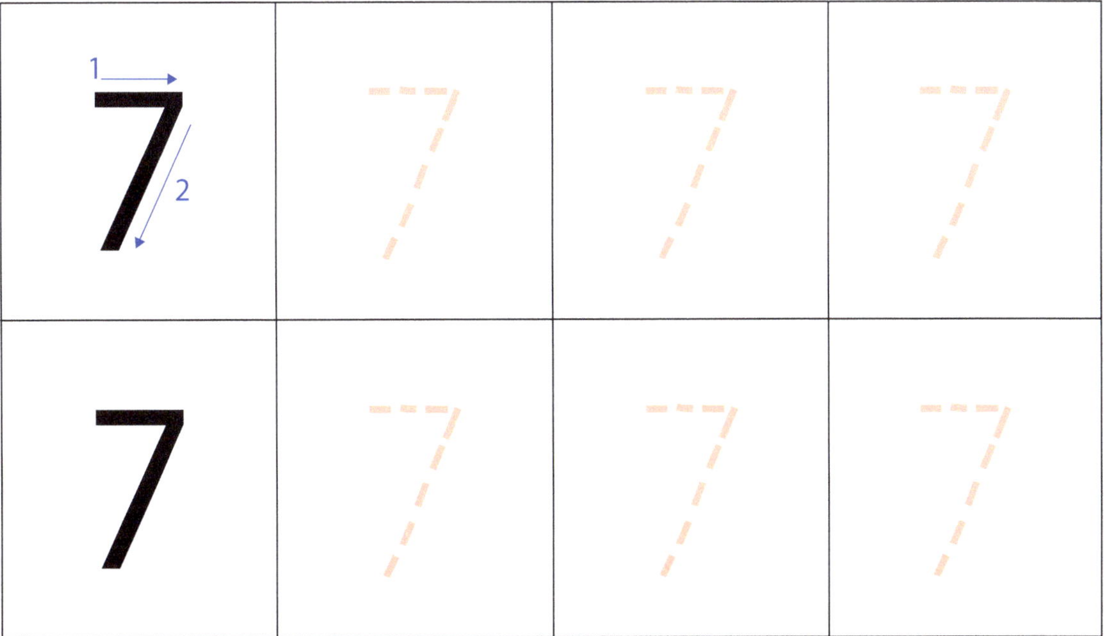

43. Food at School

Date: ___________

Objective:

To let children count the food they are going to eat. Introduce the number 8 using "add one more" method.

Method:

Teacher groups the different types of food into groups of 7. Then "add one more" equals 8.

7 add one more is 8

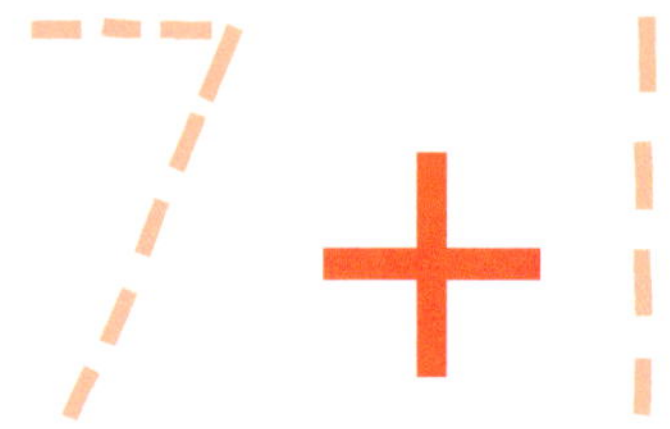

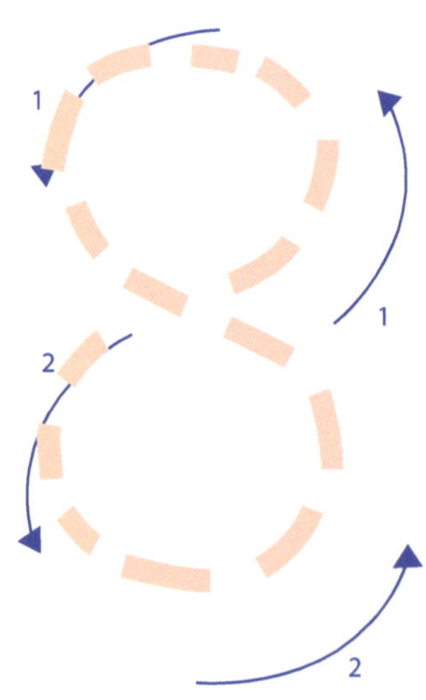

44. Food at School

Date: ________

Paste the stickers of the biscuits accordingly to the numbers shown in the boxes.

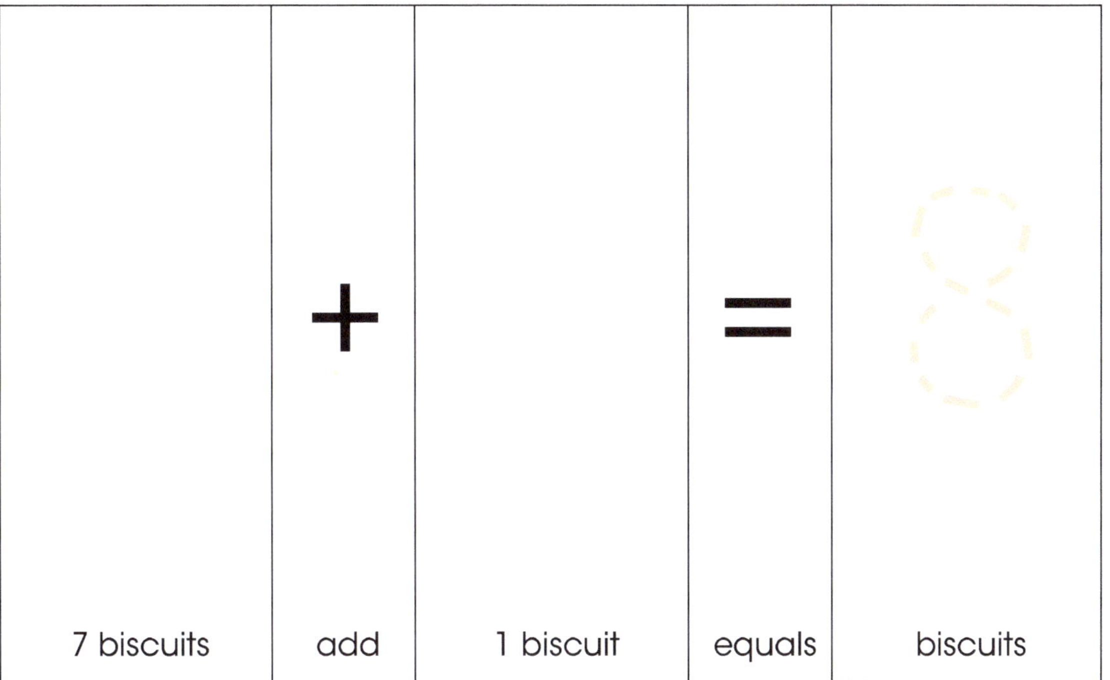

| 7 biscuits | add | 1 biscuit | equals | biscuits |

Write the number 8.

45. Food at School

Date: ______________

Objective:

To let children count the food they are going to eat. Introduce the number 9.

Method:

Teacher groups the different types of food into groups of 8. Then "add one more" equals 9.

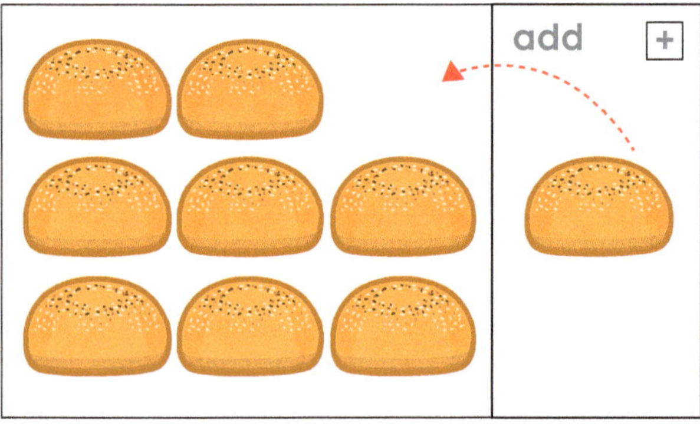

Little Ones Eduworld Meaningful Mathematics Level 1:
Activity-based Learning Book for Children Ages 4, 5 and 6 Years Old

46. Food at School

Date: _________

Paste the stickers of the food accordingly to the numbers shown in the boxes.

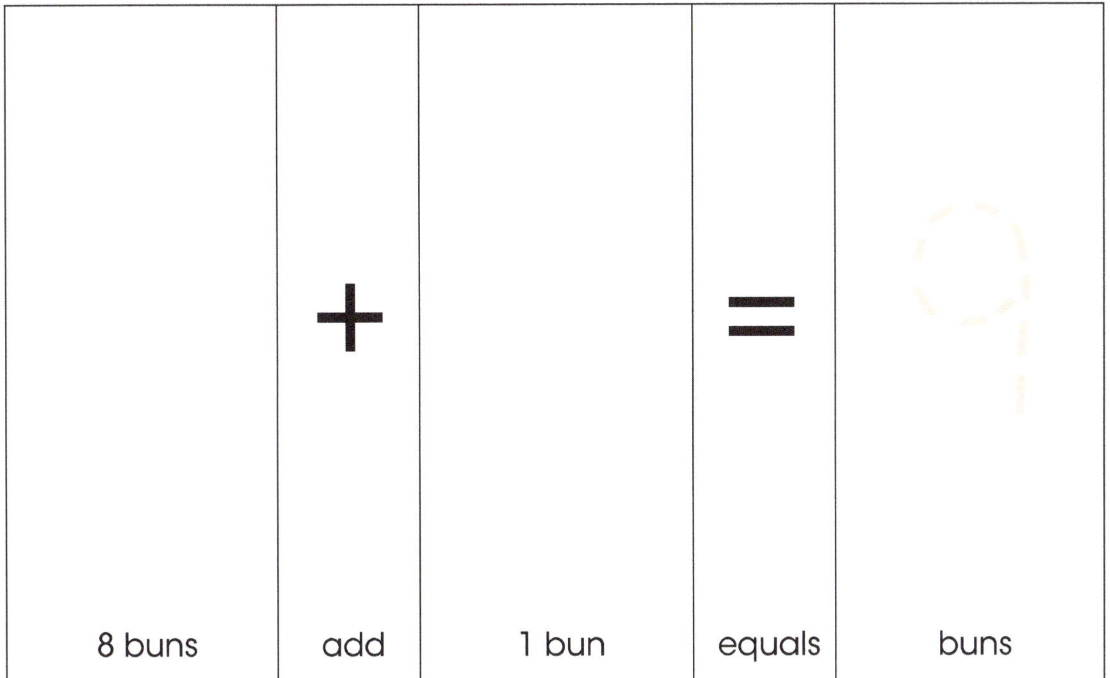

| 8 buns | add | 1 bun | equals | buns |

Write the number 8.

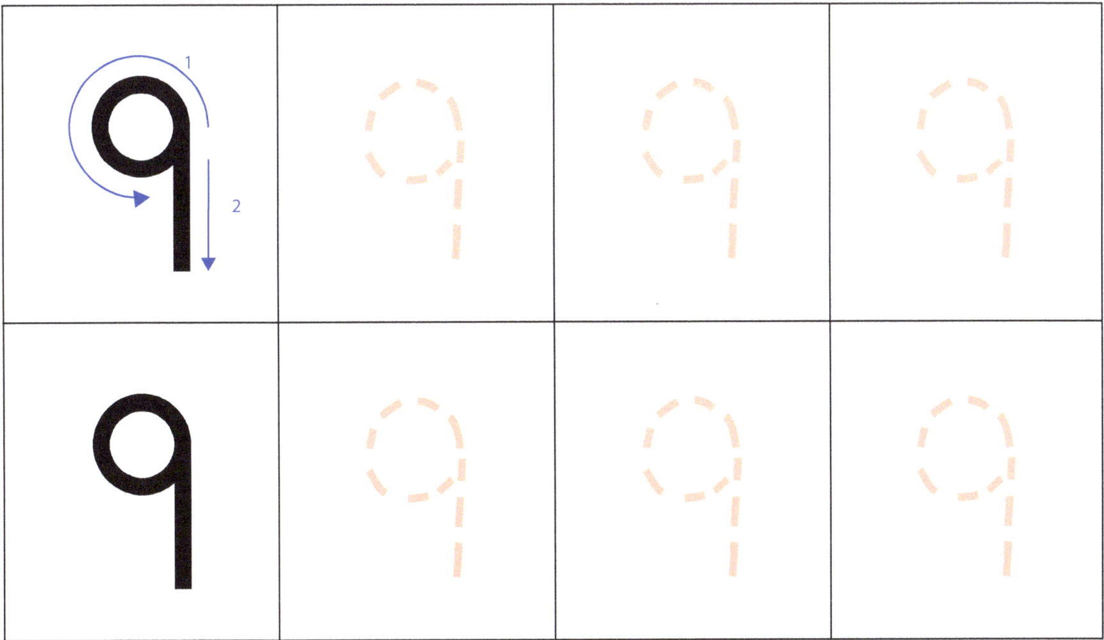

47. Candy Counting

Date: _____________

Objective:

To let children count the food they are going to eat. Introduce the number 10.

Method:

Teacher groups the different types of candies into groups of 9. Then "add one more" equals 10.

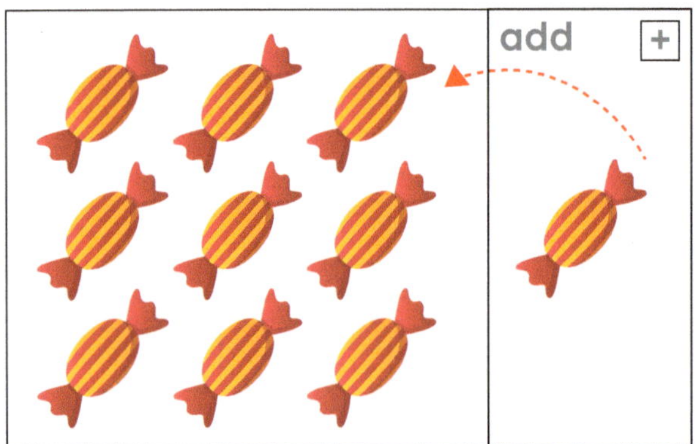

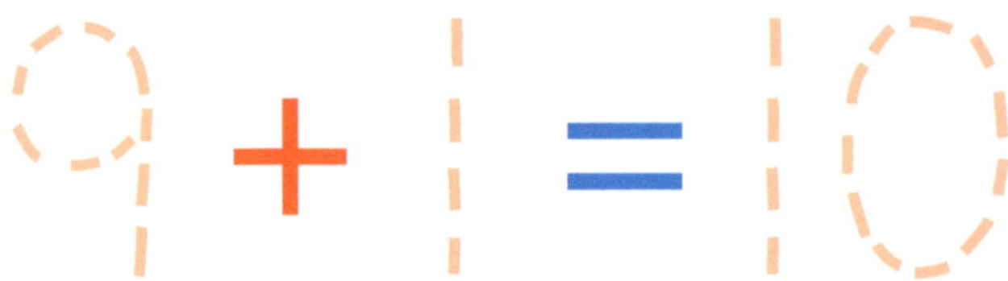

Little Ones Eduworld Meaningful Mathematics Level 1:
Activity-based Learning Book for Children Ages 4, 5 and 6 Years Old

Little Ones
Eduworld

48. Candy Counting

Date: ___________

Paste the stickers of the candies as shown in the boxes.

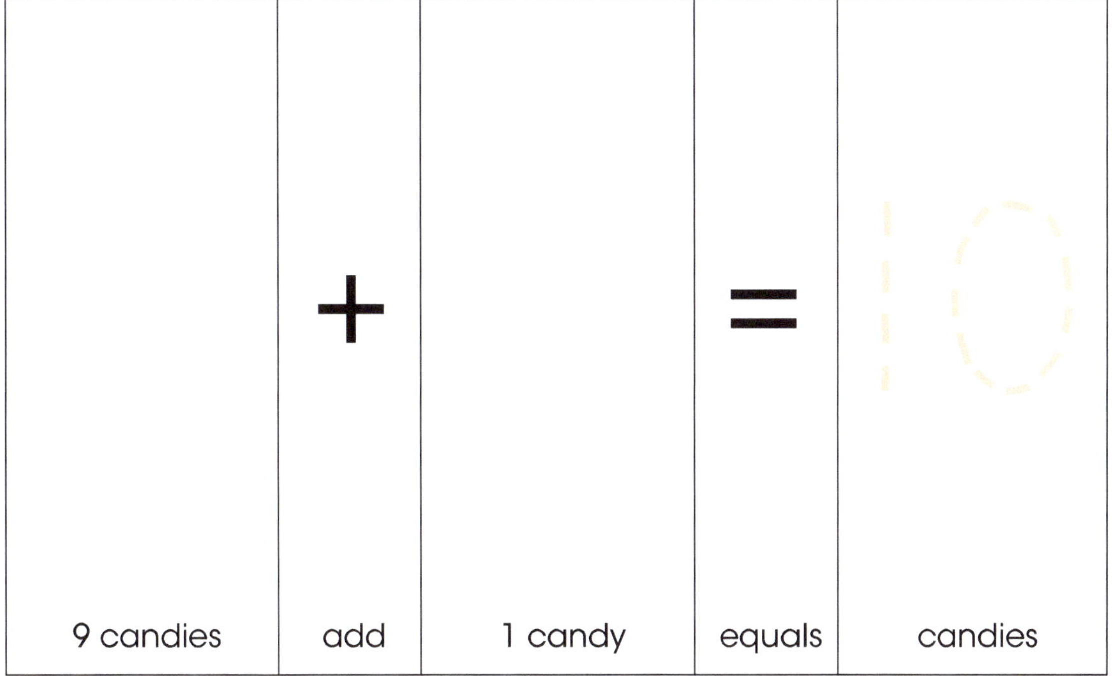

9 candies	add	1 candy	equals	candies

Write the number 8.

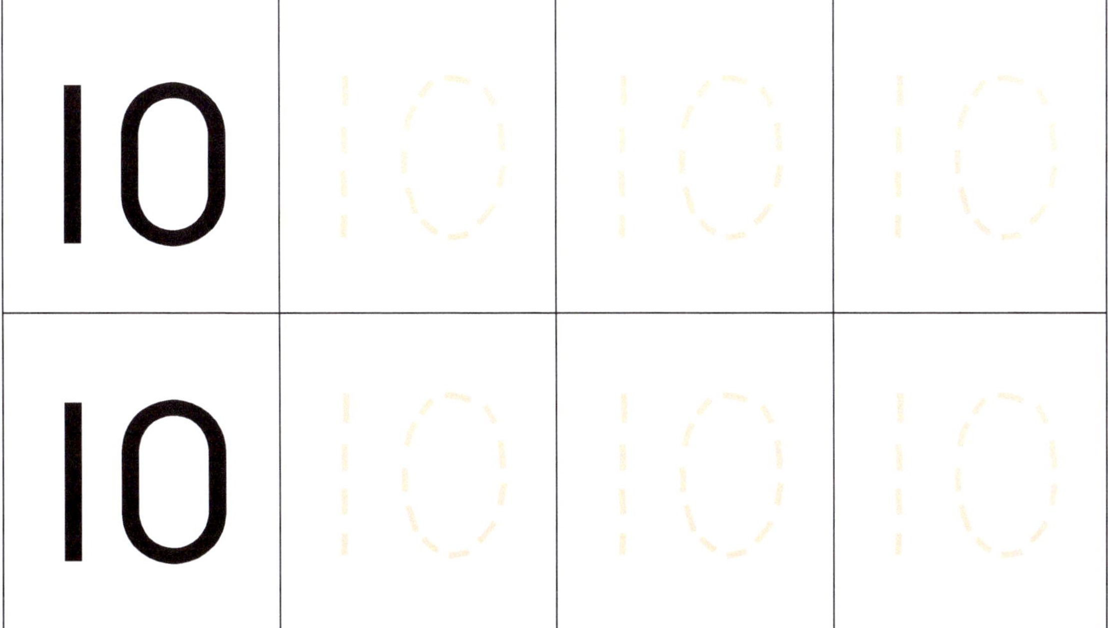

49. Crayons

Date: __________

Objective:
To form patterns of colours and to count until 10

Method:
Teacher puts multi-coloured crayons on the table. Ask the children to form patterns of 4 colours. Trace and colour the numbers according to the colour of the crayons.

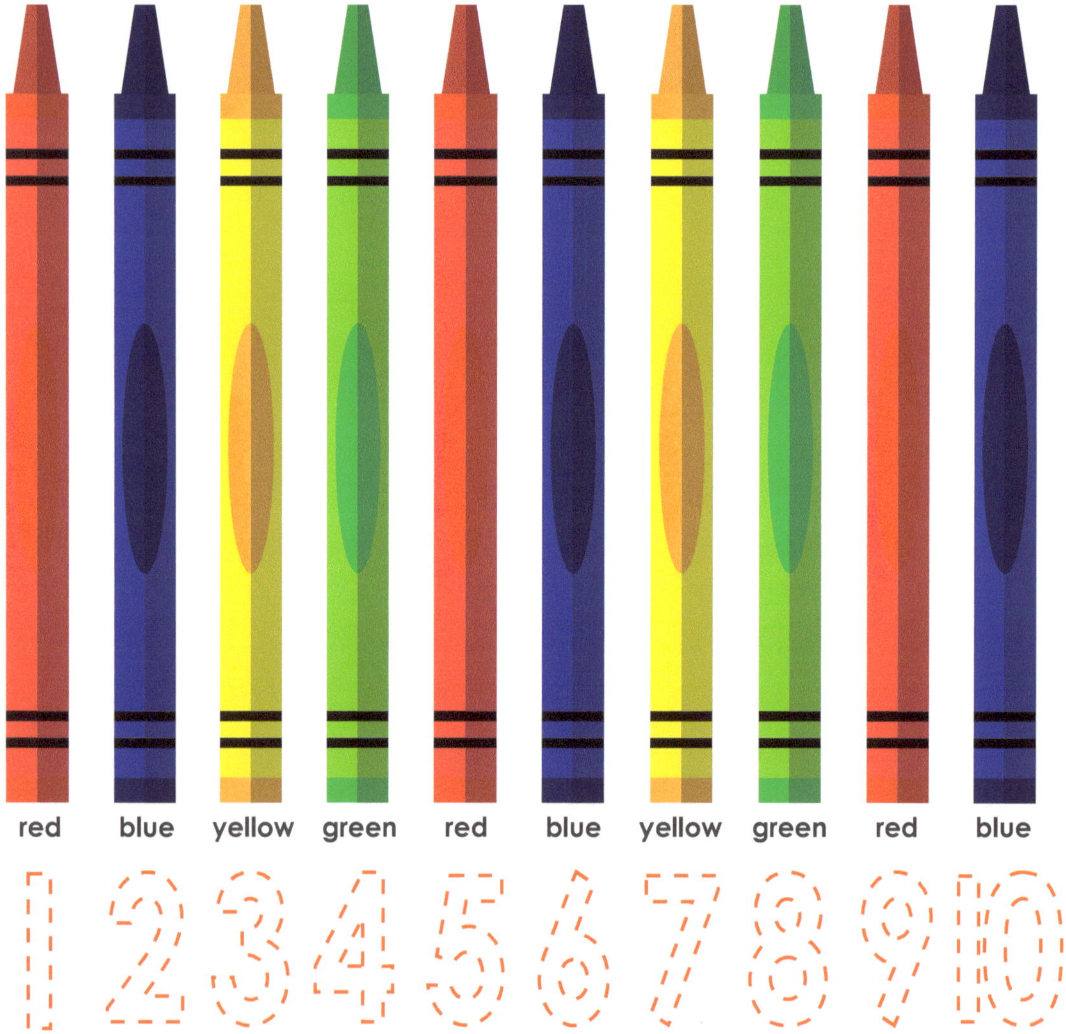

red   blue   yellow   green   red   blue   yellow   green   red   blue

1 2 3 4 5 6 7 8 9 10

Little Ones Eduworld Meaningful Mathematics Level 1:
Activity-based Learning Book for Children Ages 4, 5 and 6 Years Old

Little Ones Eduworld

CONCEPT: FORMING SET

50. Friends

Date: _____________

Objective:

To create sets of numbers using friends at school.

Method:

Teacher asks children to create groups by showing the number cards.

51. Chairs

Date: ___________

Objective:
To arrange the numbers in increasing order. (from 1 until 10)

Method:
Teacher asks children to help arrange the chairs by saying "after 1, add one more, equals 2", "after 2, add one more, 3" and so on. Line them up like the seats on a bus. Stick the number cards on the chairs. Give children tickets with the numbers on them. Let the children find their seats.

Driver Seat

Little Ones Eduworld Meaningful Mathematics Level 1:
Activity-based Learning Book for Children Ages 4, 5 and 6 Years Old

52. Exercise Books

Date: _____________

Objective:
To show the increasing order of numbers 1 until 10 using 55 exercise books.

Method:
Teacher asks children to get the number of books according to the number cards shown. Then teacher calls the numbers in an increasing order of 1 until 10. Stack the books from 1 book until 10 books and place in increasing order.

| | | | | 5 | | | | | 10 |

53. My Snacks

Date: _____________

Objective:
To let children prepare their own snacks by counting and mixing in different items based on the number cards shown.

Method:
Teacher provides peanuts, raisins, cornflakes and snack cup to the children. Teacher instructs them verbally showing the number cards. Eg: "Count 5 peanuts, 7 raisins, and 8 cornflakes". Different children get different instructions.

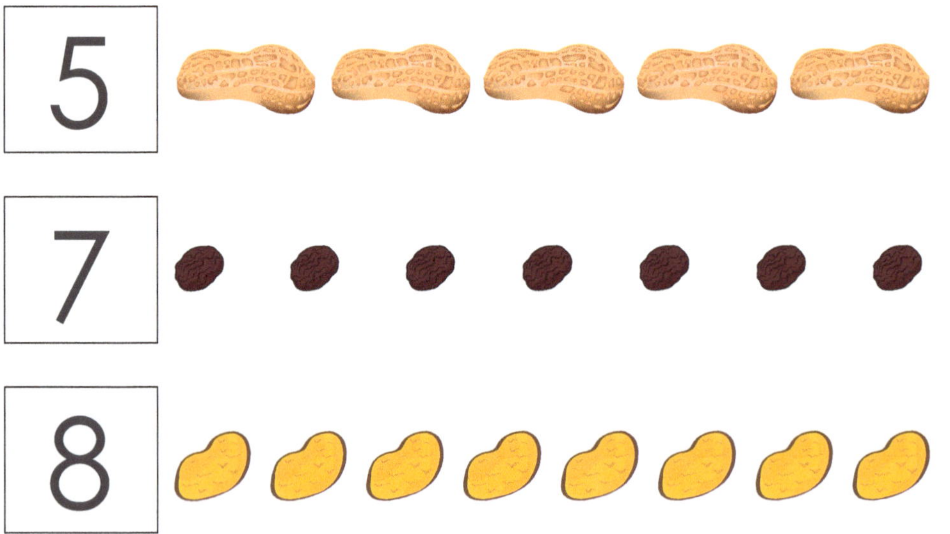

54. Numbers

Date: _________

1	1	1	1		
2	2	2	2		
3	3	3	3		
4	4	4	4		
5	5	5	5		
6	6	6	6		
7	7	7	7		
8	8	8	8		
9	9	9	9		
10	10	10	10		

55. Quantities

Date: _________

Little Ones Eduworld Meaningful Mathematics Level 1:
Activity-based Learning Book for Children Ages 4, 5 and 6 Years Old
Little Ones Eduworld

Date: ___________

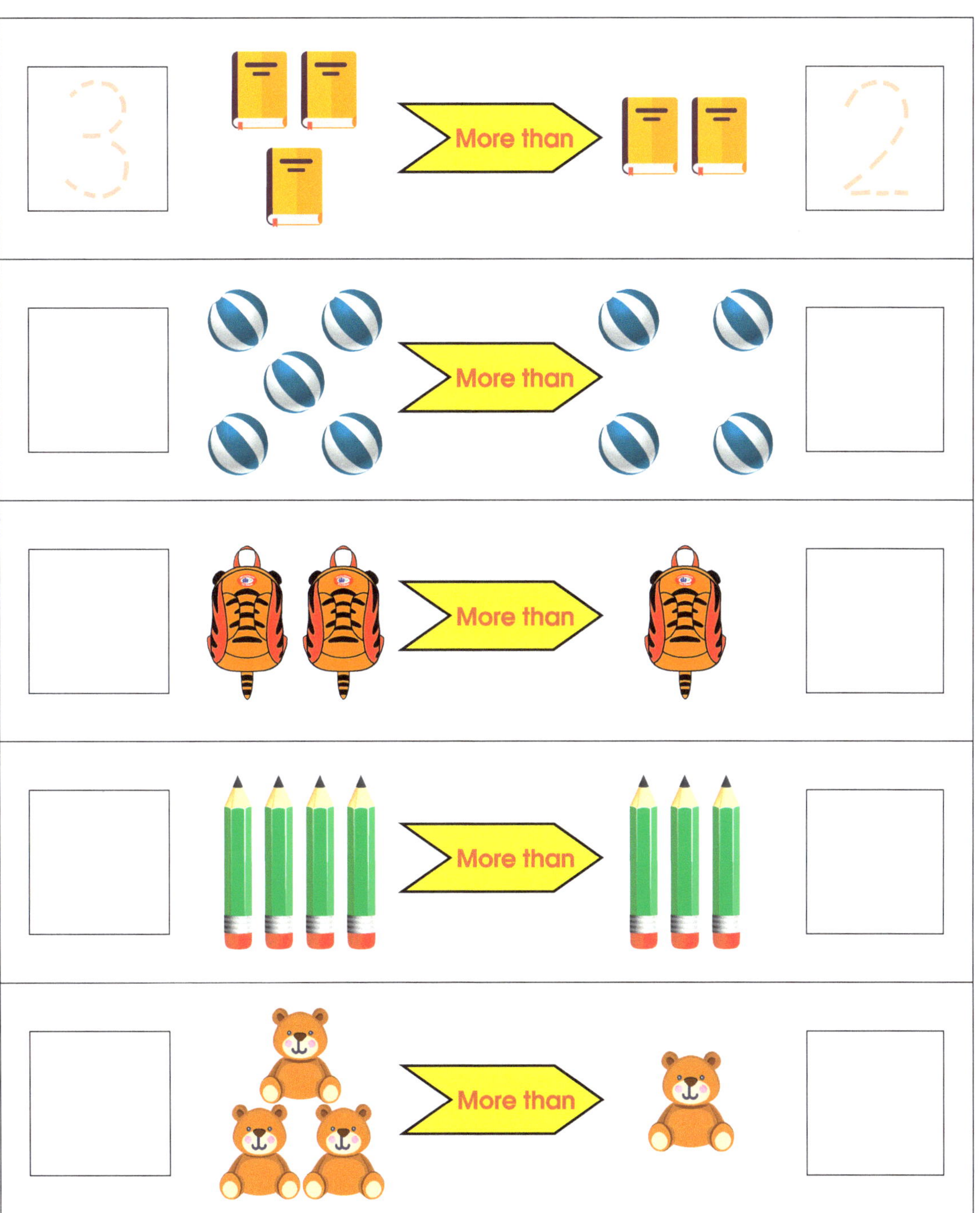

Fill in the blanks.

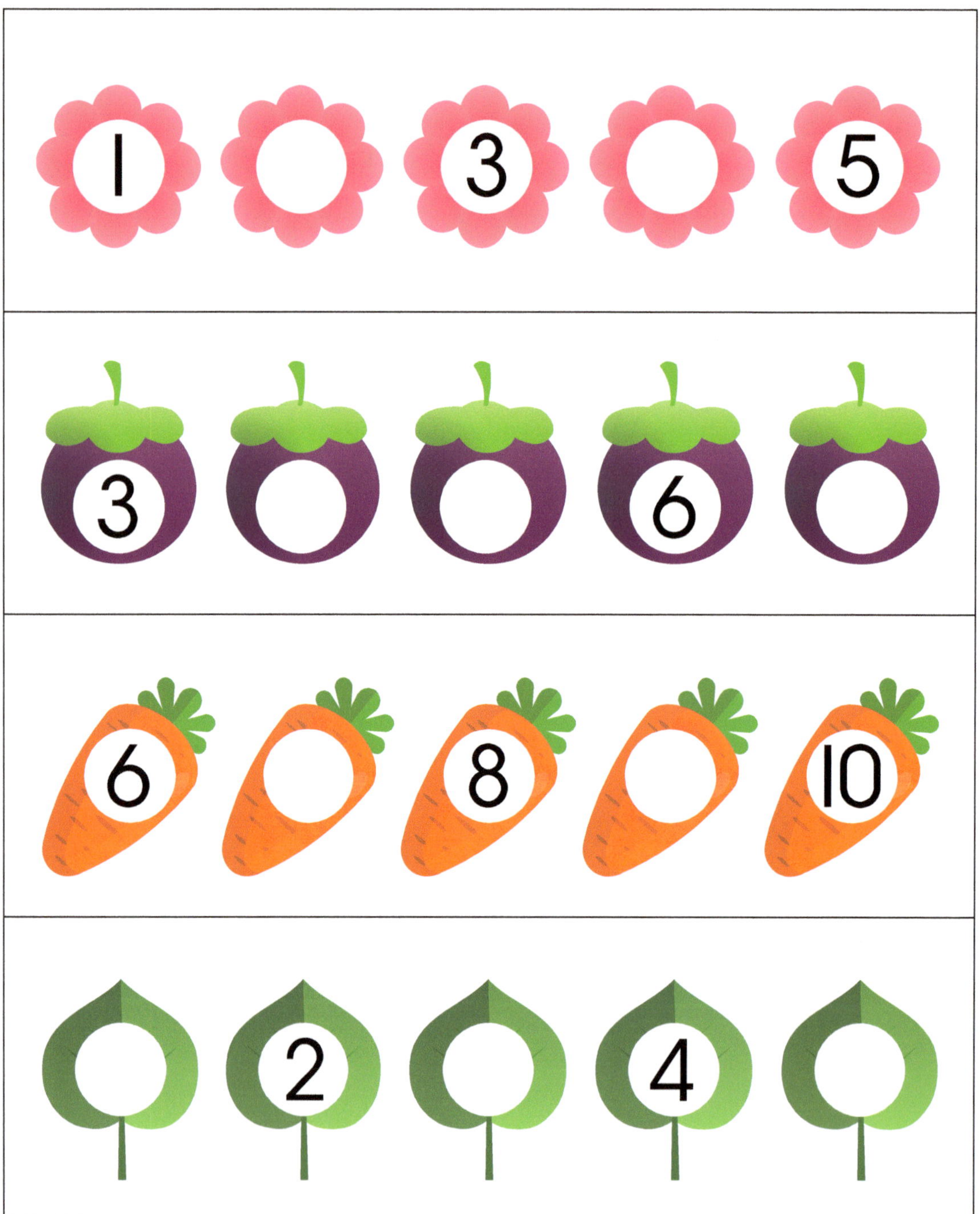

Little Ones Eduworld Meaningful Mathematics Level 1:
Activity-based Learning Book for Children Ages 4, 5 and 6 Years Old

Little Ones Eduworld

Colour the right words in the boxes for the pictures shown.

Date: ___________

Find the total.

Date: _______________

2 + 1 = ◯

4 + 1 = △

6 + 1 = ☐

3 + 1 = ☆

8 + 1 = ⬭

5 + 1 = ▭

7 + 1 = ⬡

PAGE 3

PAGE 8

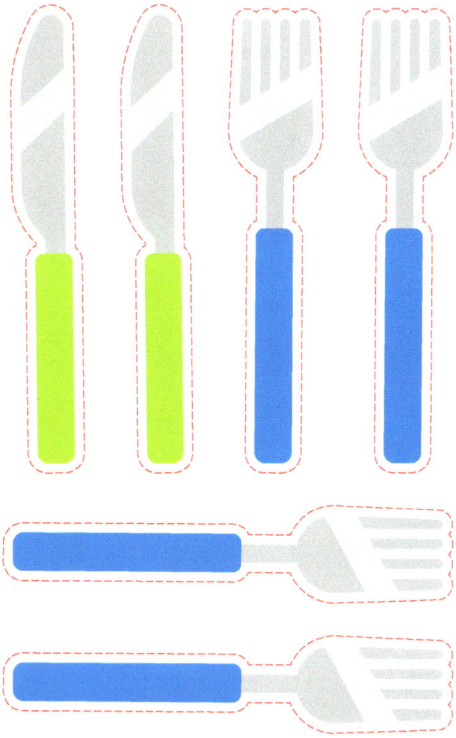

PAGE 6

PAGE 10

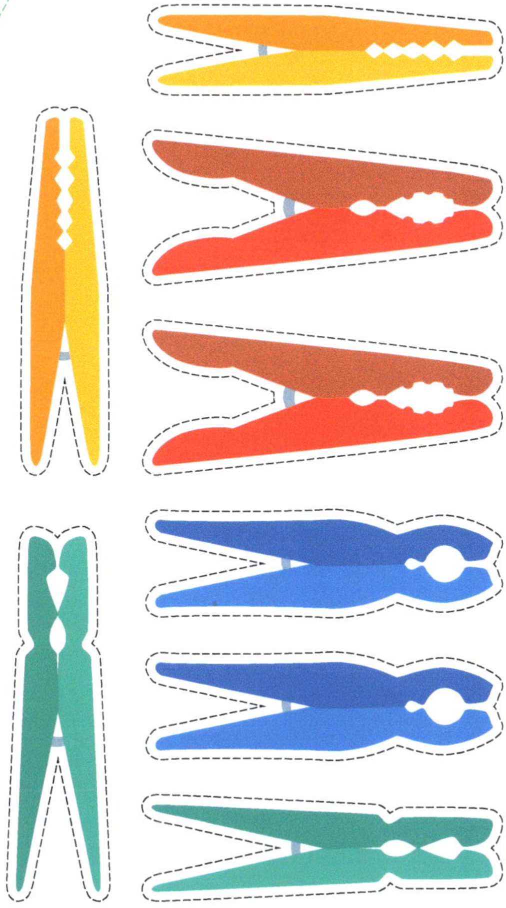

PAGE 7

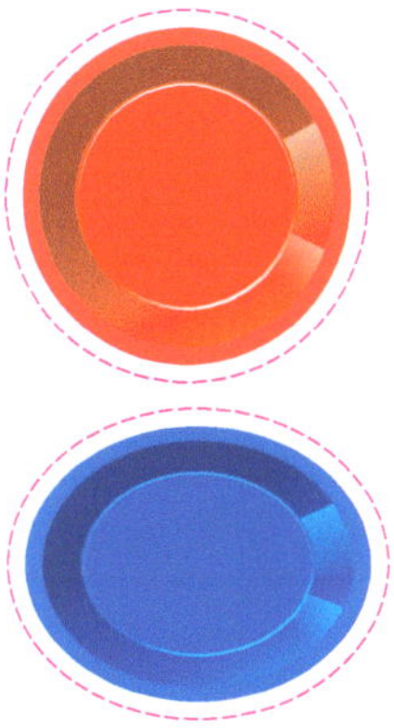

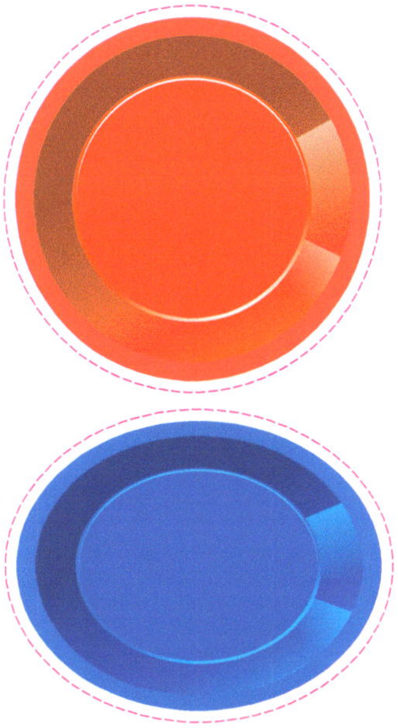

PAGE 13

PAGE 15

PAGE 20

PAGE 22

PAGE 24

PAGE 25

PAGE 34
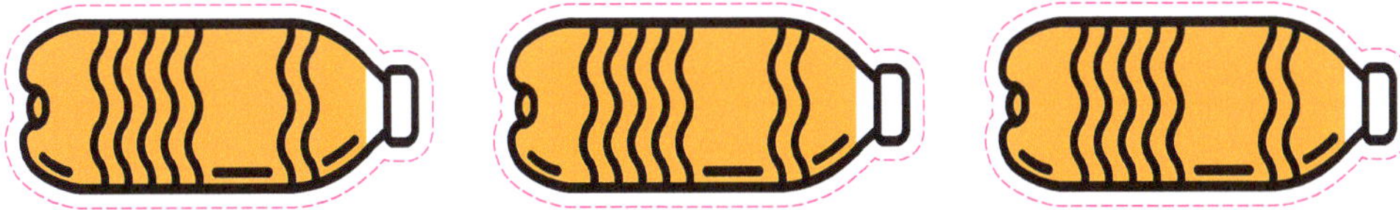

PAGE 38

PAGE 40

PAGE 43

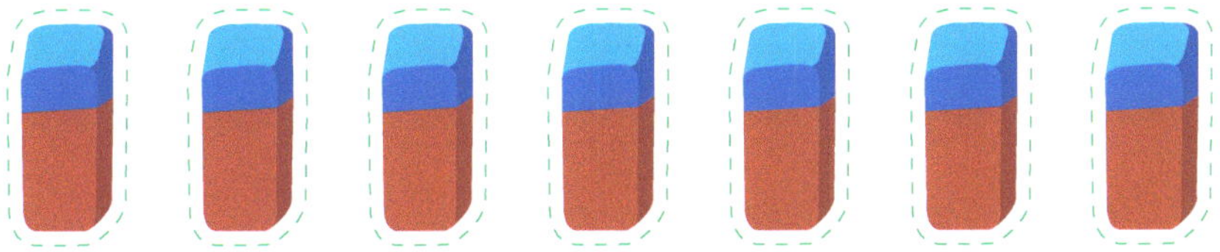

PAGE 49

PAGE 45

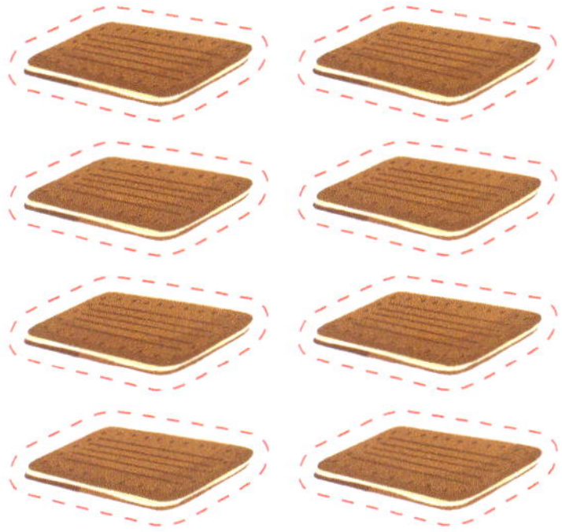

PAGE 47

FOR TEACHERS